RISE

THE UNCIVIL MENTALITY

RISE the Uncivil Mentality
Second Edition

Published by Millennial Publishing Co.
Published in Miami, Florida
Printed in United States

ISBN:
Paperback: 979-8-9861921-2-3
Hardcover: 979-8-9861921-3-0

Visit Us:
www.uncivilenterprises.com
www.millennialpublishingco.com

From the depths of hardship,
the only option is to RISE.

CONT

ENTS

UNCIVIL

/ˌənˈsivəl/ adjective

A behavior that is unconventional, non-conformist, or challenging to established norms or authority.

SPEAR FORWARD

/spir/ /'fôrwərd/

An action of relentless resiliency and perseverance towards one's goal; the willingness to decisively move toward the objective with urgency.

R.I.

Deeply rooted in every human soul lies an insatiable desire to be the best version of ourselves. We yearn for growth, to progress, and for the fulfillment of our deepest aspirations. Yet, on this journey of self-improvement, we often encounter both formidable and informidable obstacles that seem to impede our path to greatness.

But what if I told you that these barriers, though daunting, hold the key to unlocking your true potential? What if I revealed a transformative path—a path that leads you to Recognize, Identify, Seek Solutions, and Examine the very essence of your being?

The acronym R.I.S.E, was inspired from the depths of hardship, or as I dare to call it 'experience through hardship'. It encapsulates the fundamental pillars of growth and self-discovery. Each letter represents a crucial step, a life-changing revelation that will propel you towards a life of purpose, perseverance, achievement, and resilience.

R is for Recognition—the pivotal moment when you acknowledge the barrier(s), both internal and external, that stand between you and your aspirations. The first step toward transformation is the Recognition of your current state, your awareness and understanding that you hold the power to transcend it.

I is for Identify—the steadfast commitment to delve deep within yourself, to fearlessly uncover the roots of hindrance that tether you towards mediocrity. It is the pursuit of truth and the revelation of vices that impede your progress.

S is for Solution(s)—the audacious quest for answers and the relentless pursuit of growth. Armed with newfound awareness, you will forge a path to conquer obstacles. The Solutions you seek will be the bridge between the person you currently are and the person you aspire to become.

E is for Examine—the unwavering commitment to assess and reflect upon your progress. It is the foresight to evaluate the effectiveness of your efforts and to recalibrate your course when necessary. Examination is the compass that guides or informs you whether you are on the appropriate path to your destination.

This book will be broken up into four empowering phases, each dedicated to one of the fundamental pillars of growth and self-discovery: Recognize, Identify, Solutions, and Examine. Within each chapter, you will find motivational quotes from influential human beings whose messages will be the catalyst that will propel you to success during that particular phase in the transformative path. Whether accepting the mission at hand or confronting a vice, you shall R.I.S.E above self-imposed limitations and overcome any and all adversity.

R·ECO

GNIZE

As it pertains to the realm of self-discovery, one must be self-aware and the first step toward transformation is recognition. It's the pivotal moment when we stand face to face with the barriers, both external and internal, that stand between us and our aspirations. These barriers may take the form of self-doubt, external challenges, or unseen biases. The actual power is in acknowledging our current state, understanding the hurdles that lie ahead, and realizing that within this recognition lies the very essence of our ability to change.

Recognition is the initial key to unlocking our transformation because it serves as the compass that directs us towards improvement. By recognizing and acknowledging our current state, we initiate the process of change.

It's the honest appraisal of where we stand that provides the foundation for charting a new course forward. Without recognition, we risk wandering without a starting point, directionless in our pursuit of growth.

In the context of personal development, recognition is not an admission of defeat; rather, it's the embodiment of self-awareness and the first step towards empowerment. It's about understanding that the challenges before us are not insurmountable walls, but rather stepping stones to ascend. By embracing recognition, we not only dismantle these barriers but transform them into catalysts for our evolution. Think of Recognition as one of the elements embedded in a mathematical equation, and Recognition is R.

R

66

Acknowledging our
weaknesses is the first step
toward overcoming them.

Unknown

"

You have power over your
mind - not outside events.
Realize this, and you
will find strength.

Marcus Aurelius

"

To become different from
what we are, we must
have some awareness
of what we are.

Bruce Lee

We are what we believe we are.

C.S. Lewis

"

The first step toward success
is taken when you refuse
to be a captive of the
environment in which you
first find yourself.

Mark Caine

"

You cannot change what you refuse to confront.

John Spence

66

The obstacle in the path becomes the path. Never forget, within every obstacle is an opportunity to improve our condition.

Ryan Holiday

The only real mistake is the one from which we learn nothing.

Henry Ford

"

Knowing others is intelligence; knowing yourself is true wisdom. Mastering others is strength; mastering yourself is true power.

Lao Tzu

66

The first step towards change is awareness. The second step is acceptance.

Nathaniel Branden

TIFY

Amidst the landscape of personal growth, the second pivotal pillar comes into focus: Identification. This phase propels us to delve deep within ourselves, unearthing the roots of hindrance that have kept us tethered to mediocrity. It's an honest and courageous commitment to self-exploration, a journey into the uncharted territories of our fears, insecurities, and hidden potential.

Identification is the cornerstone of self-awareness—the lantern that illuminates the darkest corners of our psyche. It's the audacious act of pinpointing the habits, beliefs, and behaviors that have held us back. Through this process, we dissolve the façade that separates us from our potential selves. We peel back the layers, revealing our true ethos, vulnerabilities and all, as we lay the groundwork for lasting transformation.

This chapter's quotes are a testament to the power of identification. It's a canvas where we paint stories of individuals who ventured into their inner landscapes, emerging stronger, wiser, and more resilient. In recognizing and along with identification, we unlock the potential to transcend limitations, fostering a profound connection with our inner selves that paves the way for meaningful growth. As we traverse these narratives and absorb the insights they offer, we'll discover that the journey of identification isn't just about uncovering limitations— it's about unearthing the boundless potential that has always resided within us, because in all honesty, the power truly lies within you. Identification is another one of the elements embedded in the mathematical equation; Identification is I.

R + I

"

Knowing yourself is the beginning of all wisdom.

Aristotle

66

Identify your problems,
but give your power and
energy to solutions.

Tony Robbins

"

You are not a drop in the
ocean. You are the entire
ocean in a drop.

Rumi

The first and greatest victory is to conquer yourself.

Plato

66

The worst enemy you can meet will always be yourself.

Friedrich Nietzsche

❝❝

You should take responsibility for your own life. Period.

Jordan Peterson

66

The most important conversation you'll ever have is the one you have with yourself.

David Goggins

To find yourself, think for yourself.

Socrates

"

Your potential is determined
by your choices and
your actions.

Tim Grover

66

The moment you accept responsibility for everything in your life is the moment you can change anything in your life.

Andy Frisella

S·OLU

TIONS

Stepping into the heart of personal growth, we encounter the third pillar: Solutions—a realm where audacity meets action. Armed with the power gained from recognition and the clarity from identification, we pursue a fearless quest for answers. Solutions are the tangible bridges we build between the person we are and the person we aspire to become.

Solutions are about daring to address challenges head-on, equipped with newfound awareness and a refusal to be confined by obstacles. By seeking solutions, we breathe life into our aspirations, converting intention to action. This phase echoes with the footsteps of those who have confronted adversity and emerged victorious, each step an affirmation of the power of perseverance.

In the quotes that unfold within this chapter, we witness individuals who defied the status quo and forged their own paths. Through sheer determination, they demonstrated that the pursuit of solutions isn't a journey for the faint-hearted—it's a venture for the relentless. Solutions aren't merely answers; they are the manifestations of our commitment to growth and defy stagnation. This is the pillar of decisiveness, where actions to solve a problem, a challenge, face adversity or overcome a vice are made. In the mathematical equation, Solutions is either a positive or a negative, represented by + or -, due to the nature of Solutions can either add or subtract a solution to the mathematical equation. Thus far, the mathematical equation looks as followed:

$$R + I +/- (S)$$

"

Don't find fault;
find a remedy.

Henry Ford

"

Do what you say you're going to do, when you say you're going to do it.

Andy Frisella

"

The man who moves a
mountain begins by carrying
away small stones.

Confucius

The most effective way to do it is to do it.

Amelia Earhart

66

Action is the foundational key to all success.

Pablo Picasso

In every problem, there's a hidden opportunity.

Zig Ziglar

"

The secret of getting ahead is getting started.

Mark Twain

"

You are what you do, not what you say you'll do

Carl Jung

MINE

As our voyage through personal growth nears its pinnacle, we arrive at the fourth and final pillar: Examination. This phase encapsulates the wisdom of reflection—the practice of looking back to move ourselves forward. It's the steady commitment to assess our progress, to recalibrate our course when necessary, and to ensure that we remain aligned with our purpose and toward our goal.

Examination isn't a passive act; it's an intentional pause, purposely designed as a moment of clarity. It's the compass that guides us through the labyrinth of growth, to make adjustments if necessary. This chapter's quotes underscores the notion that the path to lasting transformation isn't linear; it's a continuous loop of growth, reflection, and refinement.

Within the narratives we explore, we find individuals who recognized the significance of examination. They discovered that the true measure of progress isn't solely in the destination but in the journey itself—the moments of introspection that shape our evolution. Examination isn't an endpoint; it's a touchstone, a checkpoint that reassures us that our efforts are aligned with our vision. Examine and re-examine, to assess and re-assess the situation or task at hand.

The RISE model in mathematical form:

$$\mathbf{R} + \mathbf{I} +/- (\mathbf{S}) = |\text{Outcome}|$$
$$\text{proceed to } \mathbf{E}$$

"

If you're not getting the results you want, change what you're doing.

Tim Grover

66

We do not learn from experience... we learn from reflecting on experience.

John Dewey

"

Your life is a reflection
of your thoughts.
If you change your thinking,
you change your life.

Louise Hay

Don't expect victory or defeat. Plan for victory, learn from defeat.

Gary John Bishop

66

An unexamined life is not worth living.

Socrates

66

Success is not final, failure is not fatal: It is the courage to continue that counts.

Winston Churchill

"

You do not rise to the level of your goals. You fall to the level of your systems.

James Clear

wisdom.

Baltasar Gracián

66

Compare yourself to who you were yesterday, not to who someone else is today.

Jordan Peterson

"

Don't wish it was easier;
wish you were better.
Don't wish for fewer problems;
wish for more skills.
Don't wish for less challenge;
wish for more wisdom.

Jim Rohn

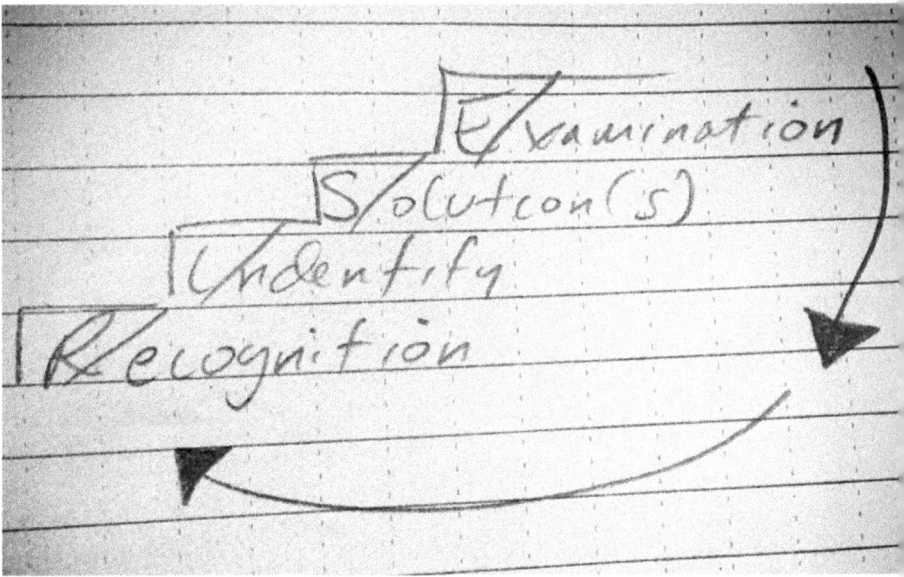

R.I.S.E Circa 2016

If you would like to know more about our publications and authors please reach out to:

www.uncivilenterprises.com
Instagram: @uncivilenterprises

www.millennialpublishingco.com
Instagram: @millennialpublishingco

About the Author

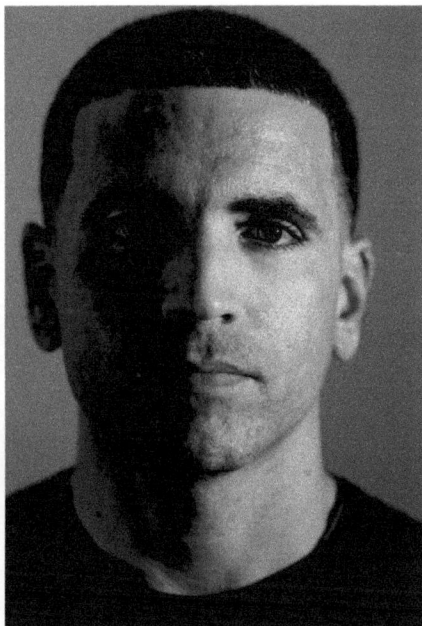

After a decade of military service, Erik founded UNCIVIL Enterprises and UNCIVIL Apparel, where he fosters the UNCIVIL mentality and celebrates American patriotism. As a firefighter, he carries his dedication to service, proving his ability to adapt and overcome challenges with courage and determination.

Erik Vidal is a true patriot, driven by an unwavering commitment to serving others and protecting his community. As a decorated veteran of the United States Army, Erik's journey has been marked by resilience and a deep sense of purpose. Through his experiences as a soldier, officer, filmmaker, and entrepreneur, he has embraced the R.I.S.E model— Recognize, Identify, Solutions, Examination—guiding him to continuously grow and make a positive impact.

Erik Vidal's life story is one of serving a higher purpose and constant self-discovery, a testament to the power of R.I.S.E to pursue one's true potential. He continues to make a lasting difference and inspire others to rise above, embrace change, and lead a life of purpose.

Notes

www.ingramcontent.com/pod-product-compliance
Lightning Source LLC
Chambersburg PA
CBHW041932260326
41914CB00010B/1264